THE MAYFLY

*In memory of a tumbling mountain stream
in the Great Smoky Mountains, and of the mayflies
that danced across the dark pools at dusk.*

ROSS E. HUTCHINS

THE MAYFLY

illustrated by
Jean Day Zallinger

Addison-Wesley

 An Addisonian Press Book

The Addison-Wesley Publishing Company, Inc.
Reading, Massachusetts 01867
Library of Congress catalog card number 75–105873
Printed in the United States of America
First printing
SBN: 201–03100–0

The stream tumbled down from the high mountains. In some places it rushed over great boulders and spilled into quiet pools where mountain trout swam in the clear water. In other places it rippled along between moss-covered banks.

It was autumn and the trees beside the stream were tinted with red and gold. In the late afternoon sun the leaves of the sourwoods and scarlet oaks looked almost as if they were on fire. Here and there, their bright colors were mirrored in the stream's dark surface.

Beyond the stream grew many hemlocks and beneath them evening shadows were already gathering. From a witch-hazel tree, a chipping sparrow sang its twilight song. No other sounds could be heard above the roar of the rushing water.

Slowly, from among the hemlocks there stepped a deer. It paused a moment, then walked down across the mossy carpet to the water's edge. Here it lowered its head and began drinking. A fish broke the surface but the deer went on drinking at the margin of the stream.

As the shadows lengthened, the deer, no longer thirsty, turned and walked slowly away through the hemlocks. All was now quiet except for the call of the chipping sparrow in the witch-hazel tree.

6

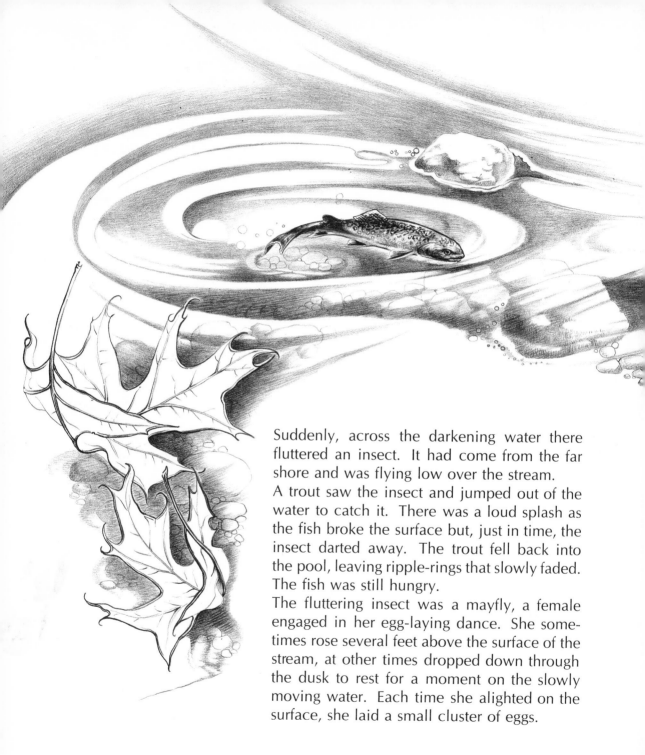

Suddenly, across the darkening water there fluttered an insect. It had come from the far shore and was flying low over the stream.

A trout saw the insect and jumped out of the water to catch it. There was a loud splash as the fish broke the surface but, just in time, the insect darted away. The trout fell back into the pool, leaving ripple-rings that slowly faded. The fish was still hungry.

The fluttering insect was a mayfly, a female engaged in her egg-laying dance. She sometimes rose several feet above the surface of the stream, at other times dropped down through the dusk to rest for a moment on the slowly moving water. Each time she alighted on the surface, she laid a small cluster of eggs.

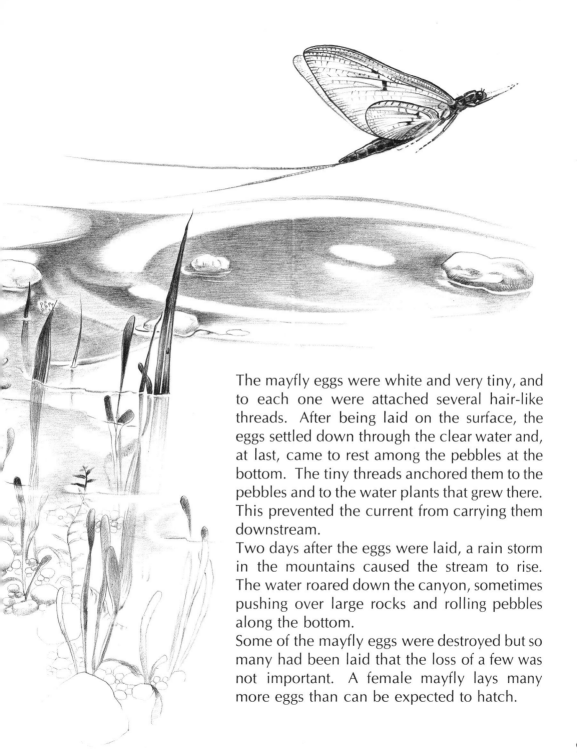

The mayfly eggs were white and very tiny, and to each one were attached several hair-like threads. After being laid on the surface, the eggs settled down through the clear water and, at last, came to rest among the pebbles at the bottom. The tiny threads anchored them to the pebbles and to the water plants that grew there. This prevented the current from carrying them downstream.

Two days after the eggs were laid, a rain storm in the mountains caused the stream to rise. The water roared down the canyon, sometimes pushing over large rocks and rolling pebbles along the bottom.

Some of the mayfly eggs were destroyed but so many had been laid that the loss of a few was not important. A female mayfly lays many more eggs than can be expected to hatch.

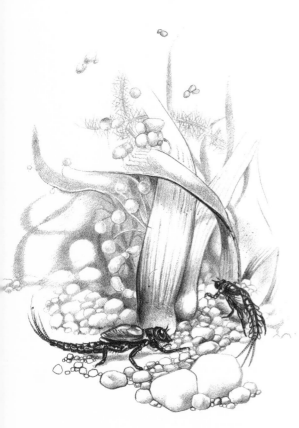

Two weeks later, the eggs began to hatch. The young mayflies that broke out of the shells were very tiny. Their bodies were made up of many ring-like segments. The young mayflies were called nymphs, and they fed upon tiny bits of plant life at the bottom of the stream. After several days the nymphs' skins became too tight. A split now appeared down the back of each one, and it slowly crawled out of its skin. The new skin was slightly larger than the old one. This was the way the nymphs grew. It was like a boy taking off a too-tight suit of clothes and finding a larger suit inside.

The days and nights in the mountains were becoming colder and colder. On some mornings the banks of the stream were white with frost. The pretty leaves of autumn had all fallen from the trees, leaving the limbs bare against the sky. Some of the leaves had fallen into the water, where they looked like bits of colored paper as they floated along.

Deep in the clear pools, the mayfly nymphs were still growing. Every few days during warmer weather their skins had become too tight, and they had shed them. After each molt, the nymphs were a little larger than they had been before. But now, as the water became colder, they were not growing as fast.

Winter came with its snow and cold. In many places the stream froze over, but its gurgling sounds could still be heard as it flowed along beneath the ice. Rabbits often hopped along the snowy banks, leaving their tracks on the surface. On cold, moonlit nights owls sometimes swept down from the hemlocks and captured deer mice that had ventured out of their warm nests.

Deep in the pools, the mayfly nymphs clung to rocks and pebbles. They seldom moved about now, and they ate very little. For them, winter was a quiet time.

13

When spring came, the snow in the high mountains began to melt. The water rushed down the canyon in torrents and overflowed its mossy margins. The stream ground the rocks together and carried fallen trees and limbs along in its swift current. In some places, great boulders were tumbled about and even rolled out upon the banks. It was hard to believe that any living thing could survive in the raging water.

The spring sun gradually warmed the mountain slopes and soon the snow was gone. Once more the stream tumbled gently down from pool to pool. Bluets and dandelions made splashes of color along the banks.

Deep in the pools, the mayfly nymphs began feeding and growing again. Every few days they stopped feeding and shed their skins.

June came, and the weather was warmer. The snowy blossoms of the dogwoods had all fallen to the ground or into the stream, and the branches were now clothed with green leaves. No longer was the stream ice-cold. Insects of many kinds were now active along the banks and beneath the water.

By this time the nymphs had molted their skins about a dozen times and on their backs there were now small pads. These pads were the beginnings of future wings and would gradually increase in size at each molt.

Along the sides of each nymph there were rows of small gills that waved up and down as the mayflies breathed. Attached to the tail of each nymph were three long, feathery bristles. These aided the nymphs in darting away when enemies appeared.

Most voracious of all their enemies were the dragonfly nymphs. They were always hungry. When a mayfly nymph wandered close to one of the dragonfly nymphs, its strange, jaw-like lip flashed out and the nymph was gone.

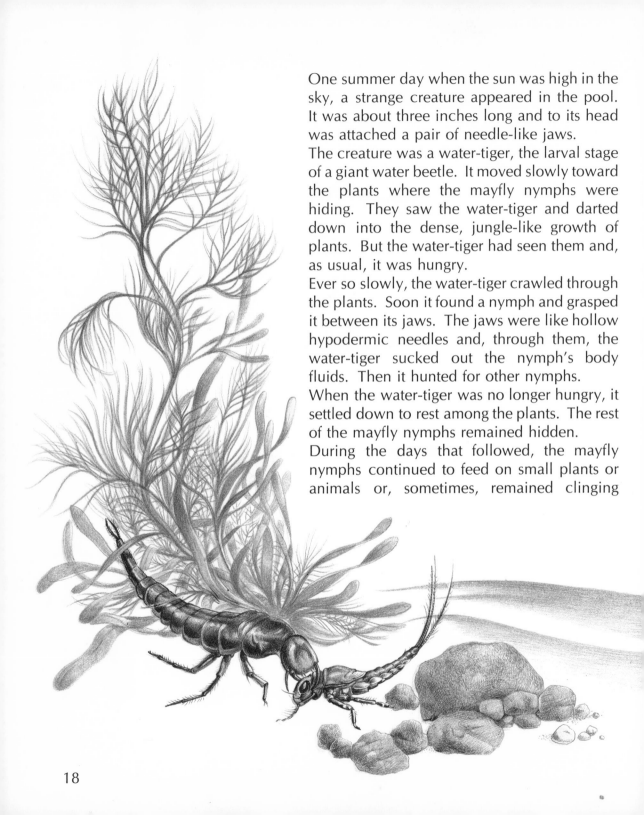

One summer day when the sun was high in the sky, a strange creature appeared in the pool. It was about three inches long and to its head was attached a pair of needle-like jaws.

The creature was a water-tiger, the larval stage of a giant water beetle. It moved slowly toward the plants where the mayfly nymphs were hiding. They saw the water-tiger and darted down into the dense, jungle-like growth of plants. But the water-tiger had seen them and, as usual, it was hungry.

Ever so slowly, the water-tiger crawled through the plants. Soon it found a nymph and grasped it between its jaws. The jaws were like hollow hypodermic needles and, through them, the water-tiger sucked out the nymph's body fluids. Then it hunted for other nymphs.

When the water-tiger was no longer hungry, it settled down to rest among the plants. The rest of the mayfly nymphs remained hidden.

During the days that followed, the mayfly nymphs continued to feed on small plants or animals or, sometimes, remained clinging

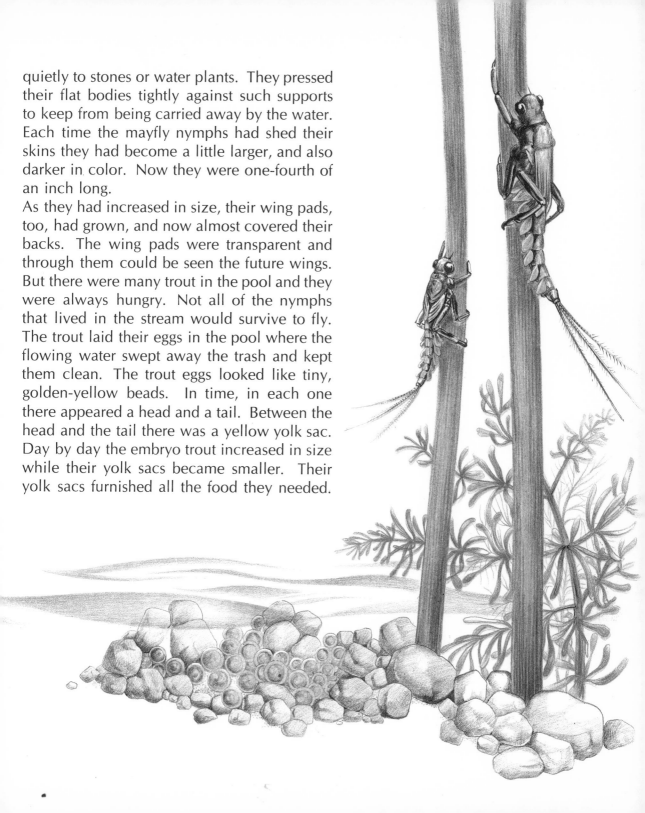

quietly to stones or water plants. They pressed their flat bodies tightly against such supports to keep from being carried away by the water. Each time the mayfly nymphs had shed their skins they had become a little larger, and also darker in color. Now they were one-fourth of an inch long.

As they had increased in size, their wing pads, too, had grown, and now almost covered their backs. The wing pads were transparent and through them could be seen the future wings. But there were many trout in the pool and they were always hungry. Not all of the nymphs that lived in the stream would survive to fly. The trout laid their eggs in the pool where the flowing water swept away the trash and kept them clean. The trout eggs looked like tiny, golden-yellow beads. In time, in each one there appeared a head and a tail. Between the head and the tail there was a yellow yolk sac. Day by day the embryo trout increased in size while their yolk sacs became smaller. Their yolk sacs furnished all the food they needed.

The young trout wiggled about over the sand among the pebbles, and a few of them were captured and eaten by water-tigers and other hunting insects.

Each creature in the stream had its enemies. In time, when the trout had grown larger, they would, in turn, devour the water-tigers. In nature the tables are often turned. But long before they were big enough to eat water-tigers, the young trout began to feed on mayfly nymphs.

A year was a lifetime to the mayfly nymphs that lived in the stream. During fall, winter, spring, and summer the nymphs had dwelled in the water. They had molted about twenty-five times and, by summer's end, were three-fourths of an inch long.

Different kinds of mayflies have different habits. Some mayfly nymphs dwell in burrows in the mud at the bottoms of streams and ponds. Others are found only in quiet water. Still others prefer to live in swift water.

Mayfly nymphs of some kinds leave the water and grow wings in spring; other kinds wait until summer. Those that lived in the mountain stream would not be ready to leave the water until autumn.

Autumn came with its shorter days and cool nights. To the mayfly nymphs in the stream, it was the time when they would leave the water.

One evening in September, thousands of them swam up to the surface. They were now almost ready to transform into winged adults.

For a while they rested quietly at the surface. They were waiting for their skins to split down their backs. This was a dangerous time. Being helpless, they were easy prey to enemies. Water-striders ran about over the water, capturing many of the nymphs. Others were devoured by minnows. Many of the nymphs were destroyed, but thousands remained.

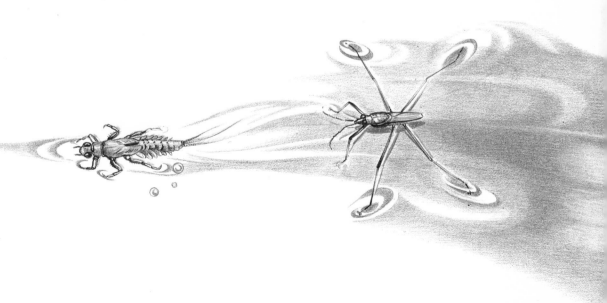

As dusk approached, the nymphs crawled out of their old skins and, at once, flew away across the water. They did not fly very fast or very well on their new wings.

One by one, they flitted away and came to rest on the leaves of nearby trees or on grass blades near the bank. They now had wings, but there was to be yet another molt before they had reached their final, adult form.

During the night, the mayflies all perched quietly in the surrounding vegetation. In the darkness they were safe from birds and other enemies.

Back in the dark stream the trout still swam slowly through the water, opening and closing their gills as the currents passed over their streamlined bodies. The sounds of the tumbling stream drifted away through the night and from the hemlocks came the lonely hoot of an owl.

When dawn came it was very cool. Mists floated over the stream and birds searched for insects in the trees.

The birds found many of the mayflies and ate them. Some attempted to escape by flying away over the water, but sharp-eyed flycatchers swooped down and captured them. The flycatchers' beaks made snapping sounds as they snatched the mayflies out of the air.

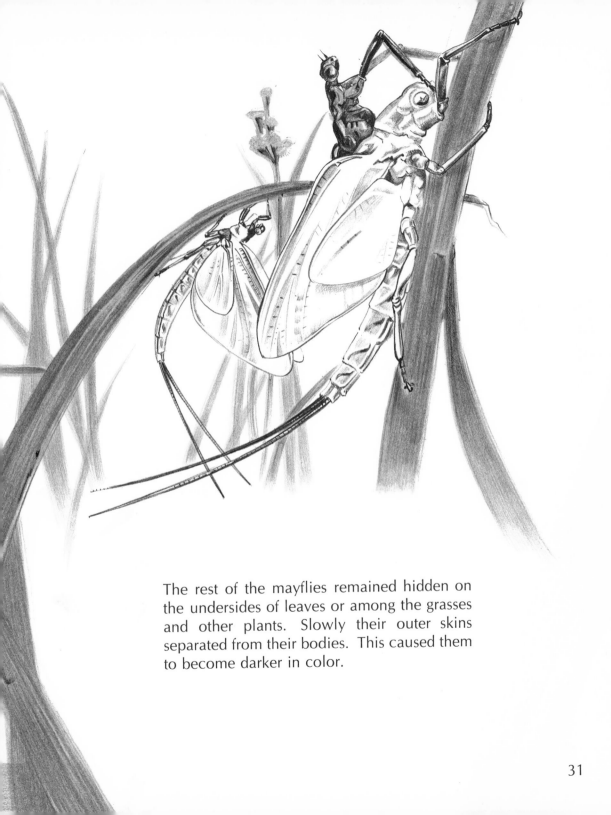

The rest of the mayflies remained hidden on the undersides of leaves or among the grasses and other plants. Slowly their outer skins separated from their bodies. This caused them to become darker in color.

After a few minutes, a seam opened down the
back of each mayfly and then the adult, winged
insect slowly crawled out. Even the tissue-like
covering of its wings was molted. The mayflies were now full-grown and would not shed
their skins again.

The adult mayflies were quite attractive. They
each had four wings that were as thin as tissue
paper. The front pair was much larger than
the hind pair, and, when at rest, the wings were
folded over their backs as in the case of butter-
flies. To the rear of each insect were attached
two slender tails.

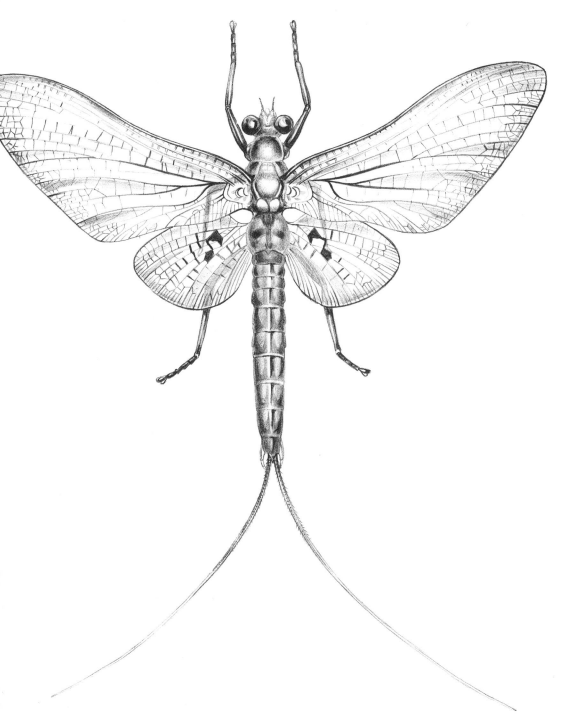

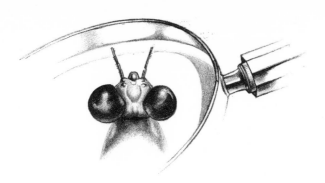

After leaving the stream and acquiring wings, the mayflies would not eat again. In fact, they did not have mouthparts and so could not have eaten even if they had desired to do so. All the food they would need during the rest of their lives was stored within their small bodies.

If you could have examined some of the mayflies under a hand lens you would have found that some individuals had much larger eyes than others. Those with large eyes were the males.

Both males and females had long front legs which they held out in front of their heads. The males' legs were longer than those of the females.

The autumn sun warmed the newly-emerged insects, but they still remained perching quietly on the leaves and grasses. In some places the plants were covered with them.

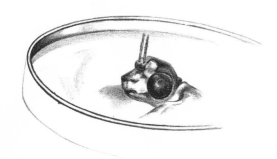

Gradually the shadows lengthened as evening twilight settled down over the pool. The time had arrived for the mayflies to dance above the water where they had lived for a year as nymphs. This would be their wedding flight, the final chapter of their lives.

The male mayflies began fluttering out of their hiding places. There were thousands of them. They held their long forelegs out in front while their tails trailed behind them like slender rudders.

Hungry trout saw the flying insects and captured many of them by jumping out of the water. After snapping up the insects they splashed back beneath the surface again.

Gradually, the males gathered in large clusters that skittered here and there, sometimes near the bank, at other times over the pool. The females remained hidden among the leaves. Then it was time for the females to join the clusters of males as they moved, light as thistledown, over the water. Into each swarm flew a lone female. She remained among the males, following them in their dancing flight.

Almost at once, one of the males in each cluster stopped his dancing flight and joined the female. Bending his long forelegs up over his head he grasped the female as she rested above him. Together they fluttered out of the cluster and across the stream.

The rest of the males continued their dance. After mating, the female mayflies gathered in small groups that danced over the pool. Dusk had now settled down and already it was dark beneath the trees beyond the stream.

The females flitted about over the water. Sometimes they rose several feet, then dropped down near the surface again.

Each time one of the females drifted down near the water, a trout leaped into the air. Some of them were captured by the trout. The rest flew on across the stream.

Now and then one of the females would actually touch the water. After barely touching the surface, she quickly rose up again. Each time, she laid a small parcel of eggs.

The eggs settled down through the water and came to rest among the pebbles and water plants.

The trout paid no attention to the masses of
eggs that drifted slowly down. They were more
interested in the flocks of mayflies that flew
about in the dusk above the stream.
At last, all the females had laid their precious
eggs. Only a few hours after acquiring wings,
their mission in life had ended.

One by one, the mayflies settled down upon the surface. Many of them were captured by the hungry trout. Others floated away in the swift water. Within a day or so all the winged mayflies were dead.

To the mayflies that had dwelled in the mountain stream, a year had been a lifetime. During most of that time they had lived and fed in the crystal waters of the pool. Many of them had been captured by voracious enemies.

They had had but a few brief hours to fly, to mate, and to lay their eggs. But those few hours had brought into being a whole new generation of mayflies, who would in turn dance above the stream on some future autumn evening.

SCIENTIFIC NOTES ON MAYFLIES

Mayflies are small, moth-like insects belonging to the order Ephemerida, a word of Greek origin meaning "to live but a day." Actually, the lives of mayflies extend over periods varying from one to three years. It is a fact, however, that after changing into the adult or winged stage they live only for very short intervals; usually a few hours or, at the most, for a day or two.

During most of a mayfly's life it lives as a wingless nymph beneath the water of a pond, lake or stream. There it feeds on dead plant material or, sometimes, captures tiny water animals. It breathes by means of feather-like gills attached to the sides of its body. When alarmed, a young mayfly, or nymph, darts away and hides beneath a stone or among aquatic plants.

They have numerous enemies. Fish capture large numbers and in many streams the young are an important source of fish food. For this reason they are of interest to sportsmen. Since trout and other game fish often jump out of the water to catch the flying adults, fishing lures of several kinds have been designed to look like them. Some of these are sportsmen's favorites.

Few people are familiar with the young mayflies or nymphs that live beneath the water, but the winged adults often attract attention when they emerge from the water in large numbers.

Often, dense clouds of mayflies are seen in the vicinities of streams or lakes. The number of mayflies in some of these swarms is almost unbelievable. Frequently they are attracted to street lights near bodies of water and by morning the dead insects are piled a foot or more deep upon the ground. During these mating flights, winds often carry them out over lakes where they perish. On following days tremendous numbers are washed ashore where they accumultate in long windrows.

After dwelling for a year in the water the adults transform into winged mayflies that flutter about in the typical swarms. It is during this brief period of aerial life that mating and egg laying occurs. After this, they all die or are soon captured by birds, fish, frogs, or other enemies.

Perhaps the most unusual thing in the life of a mayfly is the fact that, after acquiring wings, it flies away from the water and alights in nearby vegetation. After a few hours, it sheds its skin once more, including the thin covering of its wings. No other insect has this habit.

There are many different kinds of mayflies and there are some differences in their habits and life histories. They occur in almost every part of the world, except in the coldest regions. The mayflies of our story, genus Ephemerella, lived in a stream in the Great Smoky Mountains.

INDEX

ABOUT THE AUTHOR AND ARTIST

Ross E. Hutchins can write with authority on the life cycle of the mayfly, or any other insect. He was reared on a cattle ranch near Yellowstone National Park and his early interests became centered on the plants and animals of that wild country. For 17 years he was State Entomologist in Mississippi before his resignation in 1968 allowing him to devote his time to writing. The author of 18 books on nature studies and numerous articles in *Natural History, National Geographic* and other journals, Hutchins holds the Ph.D. from Iowa State University. His hobby, bio-photography, is very closely associated with his field of specialization. In fact, many of his books have been illustrated with his own photos. Recently, Mr. Hutchins was awarded a patent on a device for close-focus photography. He is a member of the American Entomological Society, Sigma XI, Phi Kappa Phi, and the Authors Guild.

Jean Day Zallinger is a sensitive artist with several children's books to her credit. As is evident from her drawings in THE MAYFLY, her delicate pencil renderings of flora and fauna lend authenticity and charm to the books she illustrates. Mrs. Zallinger is a graduate of Yale's School of Fine Arts.